Limitation Periods

Second Supplement to the Sixth Edition

D1615174

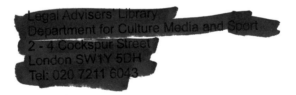

Legal Advisers' Library
Department for Culture Media and Sport
2 - 4 Cockspur Street
London SW1Y 5DH
Tel: 020 7211 6043

Limitation Periods

Second Supplement to the Sixth Edition

By

ANDREW MCGEE, B.A., B.C.L. (Oxon), F.R.S.A. of Lincoln's Inn, Barrister
Professor of Business Law, Manchester University
Barrister, Kings Chambers, Leeds and Manchester

SWEET & MAXWELL

THOMSON REUTERS

First Edition 1990
Second Edition 1994
Third Edition 1998
Fourth Edition 2002
Fifth Edition 2006
Sixth Edition 2010
First Supplement to the Sixth Edition 2012

Published in 2013 by Sweet & Maxwell, 100 Avenue Road, London NW3 3PF
part of Thomson Reuters (Professional) UK Limited
(Registered in England & Wales, Company No 1679046.
Registered Office and address for service:
Aldgate House, 33 Aldgate High Street, London EC3N 1DL)

Typeset by YHT Ltd, London

Printed and bound by CPI Group (UK) Ltd, Croydon, CR0 4YY

*For further information on our products and services, visit
www.sweetandmaxwell.co.uk

No natural forests were destroyed to make this product; only farmed timber was used and
re-planted.

A CIP catalogue record of this book is available for the British Library.

ISBN Mainwork: 9780414042988
ISBN Supplement: 9780414028647

Thomson Reuters and the Thomson Reuters logo are trademarks of Thomson Reuters.

Sweet & Maxwell ® is a registered trademark of Thomson Reuters (Professional) UK Limited.

Crown copyright material is reproduced with the permission of the Controller of HMSO and
the Queen's Printer for Scotland.

All rights reserved. No part of this publication may be reproduced or transmitted in any
form or by any means, or stored in any retrieval system of any nature without prior written
permission, except for permitted fair dealing under the Copyright, Designs and Patents Act
1988, or in accordance with the terms of a licence issued by the Copyright Licensing Agency
in respect of photocopying and/or reprographic reproduction. Application for permission for
other use of copyright material including permission to reproduce extracts in other published
works shall be made to the publishers. Full acknowledgement of author, publisher and
source must be given.

© 2013 Andrew McGee

How to Use This Supplement

This is the Second Supplement to the Sixth Edition of *Limitation Periods*, and has been compiled according to the structure of the main volume.

At the beginning of each chapter of this Supplement, the contents list for the relevant chapter is included. Where a heading in this table of contents has been marked by the symbol ■, this indicates that there is relevant information in the Supplement to which you should refer. At the beginning of the Supplement there is a contents list detailing which chapters are in the Supplement. If a chapter is missing it is because there are no updates to it contained within this Supplement.

Within each chapter, updating information is referenced to the relevant paragraph in the Main Work. Please note the paragraph numbering style has changed from 1.001 to 1–001. This has been reflected throughout the Supplement and will be changed in the Seventh Edition. Therefore within this Supplement any references to a – paragraph number relates to the Main Work paragraph.

TABLE OF CONTENTS

Contents

TABLE OF CASES

TABLE OF STATUTES

TABLE OF STATUTORY INSTRUMENTS

TABLE OF CIVIL PROCEDURE RULES

DEFINITION, BACKGROUND AND POLICY

POLICY

At the end of this paragraph, add the following text and footnotes:　　　　　**1–043**

An unusual issue of policy arose in a series of equal pay cases,[86a] where the claims were clearly out of time before the Employment Tribunal, so the claimants sought to bring them in the civil courts. There is power for the court to strike out such claims on the basis that they can "more conveniently" be disposed of separately elsewhere (i.e. in the ET). The Supreme Court held, by a bare majority, that this power should not be exercised in such a case because it is not likely to be "more convenient" to dispose of a case in a forum where it will inevitably be dismissed on limitation grounds.[86b] That of course raises the question, "more convenient" to whom? The issue has not arisen in any other context, and it seems unlikely that it could arise, because this is an apparently unique example of a claim which can be brought in two different fora, but with different limitation periods, even though the essence of the claim is identical in either forum.

[86a] See also para.27–006.

[86b] *Abdulla v Birmingham City Council* [2012] UKSC 47; see also [2011] EWHC 424 (QB), Slade J.

CHAPTER 2

THE RUNNING AND EXPIRY OF TIME

COMPUTATION OF TIME

Error by court staff

At the end of this paragraph, add the following text and footnotes:　　**2–010**

The difficult questions about when proceedings are "brought" arose again in *Barker v Hambleton District Council*,[27a] where the claim form was pushed under the outer door of the court building after close of business on the last possible day for issuing proceedings. The possibility of this had been foreshadowed in *Mucelli v Government of Albania*,[27b] where Lord Neuberger suggested,[27c] *obiter*, that this would not amount to the bringing of the action on the day when the claim form was delivered. This ignored the suggestions to the contrary in *Van Aken v Camden London Borough Council*,[27d] though that case was not cited to the House of Lords. Judge Spencer followed Lord Neuberger's comments, holding that on a day when the court office is open, the delivery of documents to the court building after hours does not amount to the bringing of an action on that day. The action is brought only when the court office is next open and the documents can be processed. A further variant on the many ways in which attempts to issue proceedings can go astray occurred in *Page and another v Hewetts Solicitors and another*[27e] where the claimants' solicitor asserted that he had sent the claim form to the court (by DX) in time for issue, but that the court office must have lost it. The Court of Appeal held that if that were the case (and it was not necessary to decide the point because this was an application for strikeout/summary judgment) then the claimants would indeed have "brought" the action within time. In effect the position is that a claimant does not have to take the risk that a claim form properly sent to the court will be accidentally lost, mislaid, damaged or destroyed by the acts of the court staff. It is sufficient if the claimant has done all that he is reasonably expected to do to deliver the claim form to the court.

27a [2011] EWHC 1707 (Admin), Judge Shaun Spencer QC.
27b [2009] 1 W.L.R. 276, HL.
27c At para.85.
27d [2003] 1 W.L.R. 684.
27e [2012] EWCA Civ 805.

2–011   *At the end of this paragraph, add the following text and footnotes:*
Harry Yearsley Ltd v Secretary of State for Justice[28a] draws attention to the provisions of the Public Contracts (Amendment) Regulations 2009,[28b] which amend the Public Contracts Regulations 2006.[28c] The amendment introduces a provision believed to be unique in English law to the effect that the limitation period provided for by the Regulations runs until the proceedings are served rather than merely issued.

28a [2011] EWHC 1160 (TCC), Edwards-Stuart J.
28b Implementing Directive 2007/66/EC.
28c Implementing Directives 2004/18/EC and 89/665/EEC.

Where remedy barred

Effect of barring of remedy

2–023   *At the end of this paragraph, add the following text and footnotes:*
In *McIntyre v Gentoo Group Ltd*[57a] the court reaffirmed[57b] the traditional rule that the Limitation Act 1980, if applicable, does no more than bar a claim or action. Cases relied upon include *Curren v Milburn,*[57c] *Norwegian Government v Calcutta Marine Engineering Co. Ltd,*[57d] *Ridgeway Motors (Isleworth) Ltd v ALTS Limited.*[57e]

57a [2010] EWHC 5 (Admin), John Howell QC.
57b Paras 62 et seq.
57c (1889) 42 Ch. D 424, CA at pp.434–435, per Cotton L.J.
57d [1960] 2 Lloyds Rep. 431 at p.442, per Diplock J.
57e Unreported; see para.17–004.

CHAPTER 3

THE RELEVANCE OF THE REMEDY

COMMON LAW REMEDIES

Declarations

At the end of this paragraph, add the following text and footnote: **3–004**
  Where a judgment is more than six years old, so that s.24(1) would pre-clude the bringing of an action on it and enforcement of it would be made more difficult by the provisions of RSC Ord.46 or, as the case may be, CCR Ord.25, it is unlikely to be appropriate to grant a declaration that the judgment is unenforceable.[5a]
  [5a] *Skiathos Touristiki SA v Protopapas and others* [2011] EWHC 1234 (QB), Dr. N. Braslavsky QC.

CHAPTER 4

CATEGORISATION

CONCURRENT RIGHTS IN CONTRACT AND TORT

Meaning of "due under an enactment"

At the end of this paragraph, add the following text and footnotes: **4–020**

In *Green v Eadie and others*[64a] Mark Cawson QC sitting as a deputy judge of the High Court held that a claim founded on s.2(1) of the Misrepresentation Act 1967 is for limitation purposes a claim founded on tort, rather than a claim on a specialty. The Court of Appeal dismissed an application for permission to appeal.[64b]

[64a] [2011] Lexis Citation 93.
[64b] Case A3/2011/3212, May 10, 2012.

CHAPTER 5

ACTIONS FOUNDED ON TORT

ECONOMIC LOSS

The solicitors' negligence cases—action by client

At the end of this paragraph, add the following text and footnote: **5–026**
   Lane v Cullens Solicitors and others[91a] is another case about when damage occurs. The defendant solicitors acted for the administrator of an estate. At their suggestion he distributed payments out of the estate on the basis of a certain understanding of the beneficial interests, even though he was on notice that there was a claim to the entire estate by a third party. That claim subsequently succeeded, and the claimant became liable for making a wrongful distribution. The question was when his cause of action against the solicitors accrued, and the Court of Appeal held that the making of the payment was the relevant date because at that point he had reduced the value of the estate and rendered himself liable to the claim for wrongful distribution.
   [91a] [2011] EWCA Civ 547.

At the end of this paragraph, add the following text and footnotes: **5–027**
   Bowling and Co Solicitors v Edehomo[93a] confirms that the principle in *Byrne v Hall Pain & Foster* (discussed at para.5–039 of the main text) applies also to solicitors' negligence cases. Where the loss is caused by an imprudent

or negligently executed conveyancing transaction, the cause of action accrues at exchange rather than at completion, because that is the point at which the client is locked into the transaction. In *Nouri v Marvi and others*[93b] the solicitors' negligence had allowed a fraudster to procure a forged transfer of land into his own name. It was held that the cause of action of the true owner accrued on the completion of the transfer, rather than on its registration, because at that point the claimant suffered a loss which was more than merely trivial.

Gallagher v ACC Bank Plc (t/a ACC Bank)[93c] is a decision of the Irish Supreme Court concerning the accrual of cause of action in a case of alleged misselling of an investment bond. Although it is of course of no authority in England, it remains interesting because the Supreme Court expresses some scepticism about the approach adopted by the English courts in relation to the accrual of cause of action in the negligent transaction cases and points out the apparent inconsistencies between the approaches in *Forster v Outred*, *Sephton v Law Society* and *Nykredit v Edward Erdman*. On the facts, though, it is held that the cause of action for negligent selling would have accrued when the bond was taken out, which is exactly the same result as the English law would have reached, whether the action was in contract or in tort.

An English case considering similar issues is *Arrowhead Capital Finance Ltd (in Liquidation) v KPMG LLP*[93d] where the alleged negligence consisted of a failure to carry out proper due diligence in relation to a company's trading activities with the result that it was refused allowance of VAT input tax, thereby causing loss to the claimant, which had lent money to the company. The claim was dismissed on the basis that the defendant had undertaken no relevant duty, but limitation questions were also considered. Having considered the same cases as were considered in the *ACC Bank* case, above, the judge summarised the law in the following propositions:

> "First, there must be actual measurable damage, although this does not necessarily mean that the damage is capable of final quantification. The mere possibility of damage is not enough.
>
> Second, the mere fact that a lender enters into a transaction by making a loan which it would not otherwise have made may, but does not necessarily, amount to damage.
>
> Third, whether the making of the loan does constitute damage depends upon a comparison (what Lord Nicholls described as 'the basic comparison') between the amount of the loan and the value of the rights which the lender acquires.
>
> Fourth, those rights will generally consist ... of (i) the borrower's ... covenant to repay and (ii) the true value of the security ...
>
> Fifth, these are all issues of fact which depend upon the evidence."[93e]

This summary appears to be a concise and accurate attempt at reconciling the otherwise apparently conflicting lines of authority.

[93a] [2011] EWHC 393 (Ch), Roth J.
[93b] [2010] EWCA Civ 1107.
[93c] [2012] IESC 35.
[93d] [2012] EWHC 1801, Stephen Males QC.
[93e] Paragraphs 76–80.

Sins of omission

At the end of this paragraph, add the following text and footnotes: **5–030**

The principles discussed in this paragraph were further examined in *Pegasus Management Holdings SCA and another v Ernst & Young (a firm) and another*,[100a] where the defendant accountants had negligently failed to give proper tax advice, with the result that the claimant was exposed to a significant risk of future adverse tax consequences and had his commercial freedom of action somewhat reduced. The Court of Appeal stressed that it is always a question of fact whether a particular piece of negligence has caused actual loss, but upheld the judge's conclusion that there was in this case sufficient detriment to amount to actual loss and set time running.[100b]

[100a] [2010] EWCA Civ 181.

[100b] See also *Boycott v Perrins Guy Williams and others* [2011] All E.R. (D) 113 (Oct), Vos J.

PROCEDURAL QUESTIONS

Evidential aspects

At the end of this paragraph, add the following text and footnote: **5–064**

See also *Legal Services Commission v Henthorn*,[174a] where it was held that the right of the Legal Services Commission to recover payments on account which proved to be excessive arose on the date when the assessment of the assisted party's costs finally established that the payments had been excessive, rather than on the making of the payments or the completion of the work.

[174a] [2011] EWHC 258 (QB), Judge Anthony Thornton QC, reversed by the Court of Appeal [2011] EWCA Civ 1415.

THE LATENT DAMAGE ACT 1986

THE LATENT DAMAGE ACT 1986

Relevant knowledge

"Attributable"

At the end of this paragraph, add the following text and footnote: **6–014**

Where a claimant wrote a letter to a building contractor indicating the existence of problems arising from work done by that contractor and suggesting the need to make a claim in respect of his losses if the problem was not speedily resolved, that was sufficient evidence that he knew that the problems were attributable to the contractor's negligence; the starting date had therefore been reached.[34a]

[34a] *Eagle v Redlime Ltd* [2011] EWHC 838 (QB), Eder J.

Fact and law

At the end of this paragraph, add the following text and footnote: **6–017**

Where the claimant should have been advised to enter into a property purchase on terms of a joint tenancy with an agreement that it could not be severed, but was in fact not given such advice and instead entered into a joint tenancy which was severable, his cause of action accrued on the completion of the purchase because he suffered discernible loss at that stage. Moreover, he had the necessary knowledge for the purposes of s.14A as soon as he realised that he had not been given this advice and that this had had adverse consequences for him—he did not need to know that the solicitors had been negligent.[42a]

[42a] *Boycott v Perrins Guy Williams* [2011] EWHC 2969 (Ch), Vos J.

Fraud

6–028   *At the end of this paragraph, add the following text and footnote:*
Williams v Lishman, Sidwell, Campbell & Price Ltd[60a] concerned the
relationship between s.14A and s.32, but is dealt with below under s.32.
    [60a] [2010] EWCA Civ 418.

CHAPTER 7

THE CONSUMER PROTECTION ACT 1987

THE LONGSTOP

'Supply' and 'putting into circulation'

At the end of this paragraph, add the following text and footnotes: **7–015**

Following the decision of the ECJ in *O'Byrne v Sanofi Pasteur MSD Ltd* the case returned to the English courts. Teare J. allowed the claimant's application for substitution of APSA in place of APSMD, pursuant to s.35(5)(b) and (6)(a) of the Limitation Act 1980 and r.19.5(3)(a) of the CPR, on the ground that the claimant had named APMSD as the defendant in mistake for APSA.[23a] APSA's appeal to the Court of Appeal was dismissed.[23b] The House of Lords granted APSA leave to appeal but at the hearing before the House some differences arose as to the effect of the ECJ judgment. A majority of the House took the view that it was clear that the European Court was saying that, in some circumstances, proceedings, which are obviously intended to be proceedings against the producer but which use the wrong name, can properly be treated by national procedural law as having been proceedings against the producer. The majority considered that this would have been the proper approach in the circumstances in the present case and so they would have dismissed APSA's appeal. But, because this was not the unanimous view of the appellate committee as to the effect of the judgment of the European Court, the House of Lords referred the case to Luxembourg for a second time.[23c] The Grand Chamber ruled on this reference in *Aventis Pasteur SA v OB*[23d] in the following terms:

"Article 11 of Council Directive 85/374/EEC of 25 July 1985 on the approximation of the laws, regulations and administrative provisions of the Member States concerning liability for defective products must be interpreted as precluding national legislation, which allows the substitution of one Defendant for another during proceedings, from being applied in a way which permits a 'producer', within the meaning of Article 3 of that directive, to be sued, after the expiry of the period prescribed by that article, as Defendant in proceedings brought within that period against another person."

The effect of this is that once 10 years have passed since a producer put a product into circulation, that producer cannot be sued, unless proceedings have been taken against it within the 10-year period. Consequently, a rule of national law which allows the substitution of one defendant for another during proceedings cannot, under Directive 85/374, be applied in a way which permits such a producer to be sued, after the expiry of that period, as defendant in proceedings brought within that period against another person.[23e]

It makes no difference if the failure to sue a particular producer within the relevant 10-year period had been due to some mistake on the claimant's part. Even in that event what mattered was that the 10 years had expired without that producer having been sued. So it could not be substituted as defendant after the 10 years were up.[23f]

It necessarily followed that the claimant could not use s.35 of the Limitation Act 1980 as a basis for substituting APSA for APMSD as the defendant. The claimant therefore fell back on a second argument based on a further answer given by the ECJ on the second reference. The Court ruled that art.11 must be interpreted as not precluding a national court from holding that, in the proceedings instituted within the period prescribed by that article against the wholly owned subsidiary of the 'producer', within the meaning of art.3(1) of Directive 85/374, that producer can be substituted for that subsidiary if that court finds that the putting into circulation of the product in question was, in fact, determined by that producer. The claimant sought to argue that this exception would apply here because the putting into circulation of the product happened when it was transferred from APSA (manufacturer) to APMSD (distributor) and that was obviously determined by APSA. There is an obvious flaw in this argument, namely that such a transfer will always be determined by the manufacturer. The only sensible interpretation of the Court's ruling is that the transfer to which it refers is the transfer by the distributor to its own customer.

So the position in relation to the 10-year time-bar may now be regarded as settled. Once the 10 years have expired, there can be no substitution of a new party, unless that party was in fact the one which caused the product to be put into general circulation. It is not enough for this purpose to show that the distributor was a subsidiary of the manufacturer, though that will no doubt be a relevant consideration.

[23a] *O'Byrne v Aventis Pasteur MSD Ltd* [2007] 1 W.L.R. 757.
[23b] [2008] 1 W.L.R. 1188.
[23c] [2008] 4 All E.R. 881.
[23d] Case C-358/08, unreported, December 2, 2009.
[23e] At para.44.
[23f] At para.48.

PERSONAL INJURIES AND DEFAMATION

PERSONAL INJURIES

The basic rule

At the beginning of this paragraph, add the following text and footnotes:　　**8–005**
Where a claimant had been diagnosed with pleural plaques but not asbestosis, he did not at that point have a cause of action for personal injury in the light of the decision of the House of Lords in *Johnston v NEI International Combustion Ltd; Rothwell v Chemical and Insulating Co Ltd; Topping v Benchtown Ltd (formerly Jones Bros Preston Ltd)*.[5a] His solicitors at that point had therefore not been negligent in failing to bring an action within three years of the diagnosis.[5b]

[5a] [2007] 4 All E.R. 1047.

[5b] *Preston v BBH Solicitors* [2011] All E.R. (D) 51 (Oct); affirmed by the Court of Appeal [2011] EWCA Civ 1429.

The date of knowledge

Knowledge

At the end of this paragraph, add the following text and footnotes:　　**8–017**
In relation to constructive knowledge in s.14(3) of the Limitation Act 1980 the Court of Appeal in *London Strategic Health Authority (Successor body in law for the Queens Charlotte's Maternity Hospital) v Whiston*[44a] held that the test is properly to be regarded as an objective one, following the decision of the House of Lords in *Adams v Bracknell Forest Borough Council*.[44b]

[44a] [2010] EWCA Civ 195.

[44b] [2004] UKHL 29, [2005] 1 A.C. 76, [2004] 3 All E.R. 897.

8–021   *At the beginning of this paragraph, add the following text and footnote:*
Where a claimant was told that he might have mesothelioma and that if he did, it would result from contact with asbestosis, that was not sufficient to fix him with knowledge that in fact he had pleural thickening, particularly given that he was subsequently told that he did not have mesothelioma.[51a]
    [51a] *Lloyd & Co Ltd v Hoey* [2011] EWCA Civ 1060.

Attributability

8–026   *At the end of this paragraph, add the following text and footnote:*
Ministry of Defence v AB raises fundamental questions about the application of s.14(3), in particular the extent to which claimants can rely on the fact that they would not until recently have been likely to get medical advice to the effect that their condition was attributable to the act or omission in question even though the evidence is that they nevertheless believed that it was so attributable. As a matter of statutory construction the question turns on the meaning of the phrase 'knows that it is attributable'. The concept of knowledge is a difficult one, because there are few things in the world which can be known with absolute certainty. The Court of Appeal held that there is 'knowledge' for these purposes where the claimant has an honest and reasonable belief that the injury is attributable to the relevant act or omission. In March 2012 the Supreme Court, by a 4:3 majority, dismissed the claimants' appeal, holding that reasonable belief in attributability is sufficient to set time running.[76a] This was the first time that this question had been considered at the highest judicial level, and it is interesting to note that there was a deep division of judicial opinion. The judgments are not easy to summarise briefly, but the following points may be helpful. The argument is in essence whether 'knowledge' for the purposes of the section has to be founded on strong objectively justified belief, or whether it is sufficient that the claimant does in fact believe that his injury is attributable to the alleged act or omission. One obvious difficulty is that the section refers to 'knowledge' which is, as a matter of language, clearly different from belief. However, 'knowledge' in a strict sense is very difficult to achieve in such cases, though belief is easier to acquire. If the section referred here to 'belief' then this problem of interpretation would not exist (and in *AB v Ministry of Defence* the claimants would clearly have been time-barred). The question is whether the concept of knowledge can and should be watered down somewhat in this context. The majority hold that it is necessary as a matter of policy to hold that time begins to run once the claimant has a belief, justified by at least some degree of evidence, that his injury is attributable to the defendant's act or omission. The minority, clearly seeking a version which is more claimant-friendly, seek to say that knowledge must be based on clear and objectively justified evidence. The debate about the choice between these two interpretations will no doubt continue, but so far as substantive law is concerned, the answer is for the foreseeable future clear – once the claimant has a strong belief that his injury is attributable to the defendant's act or omission, he satisfies the attributability part of the test for the date of knowledge.
    [76a] [2012] UKSC 9.

Disapplication of section 12

At the end of this paragraph, add the following text and footnotes: **8–037**
Mutua v Foreign and Commonwealth Office[104a] concerned allegations of torture against British servicemen going back as far as the 1950s. Issues of limitation inevitably arose. The facts and context of the case are, as the judge commented, apparently like no other case ever recorded in this country. However, to an extent the s.33 considerations, particularly those relating to a fair trial, are in principle the same as in any s.33 case. Perhaps the unique points to come out of this case are the judge's conclusions that neither the ECHR[104b] nor public international law more generally[104c] is of any assistance in determining this case. It may be observed that it does not necessarily follow that neither of these will ever be relevant. The question of the extent to which limitation periods generally are consistent with the right to a fair trial remains an open one.[104d]

[104a] [2012] EWHC 2678 (QB), McCombe J.
[104b] Paras 141–153.
[104c] Paras 154–159.
[104d] See for example *Stubbings v Webb*, discussed at para.8–009 of the main text.

Appellate courts

At the end of this paragraph, add the following text and footnotes: **8–040**
For further confirmation of the weight to be attached to the decision of the first instance judge in relation to s.33 see *AB v Ministry of Defence*[122a] and *Burgin v Sheffield CC*.[122b]

[122a] [2010] EWCA Civ 1317 at para.94, per Smith L.J.
[122b] [2005] EWCA Civ 422 at para.16, per Clarke L.J.

The relevant factors

At the end of this paragraph, add the following text and footnotes: **8–043**
In a case where resolution of the dispute turns on establishing the employment practices of the defendant many years in the past, the fact that the claimant is deceased and so not available to be cross-examined may be an insuperable obstacle to a fair trial and may thus be a strong factor against the exercise of the s.33 discretion.[132a] For a case where a s.33 application was dismissed on the basis that the passage of time had made a fair trial impossible see *HBL v Metropolitan Borough of Wirral*.[132b]
Section 33(3)(b) is concerned mostly with prejudice occurring after the expiry of the primary limitation period, rather than prejudice within that period. The question whether there can still be a fair trial is the most important question under s33.[132c]

[132a] *Hinchliffe (Executor of the Estate of Aubrey Whitehead, deceased) v Corus UK Ltd* [2010] EWHC 2871 (QB).
[132b] [2011] All E.R. (D) 61 (Dec).
[132c] *Roberts v Commissioner of Police of the Metropolis* [2012] EWCA Civ 799.

Case law developments

8–053   *At the end of this paragraph, add the following text and footnotes:*

In *EB v Haughton*[167a] Slade J. made some comments on the approach to be taken when considering whether to disapply the limitation period, particularly in cases of alleged sexual abuse, relying to some extent on the observations of Lord Brown in *A v Hoare*.[167b]

Whether or not it will be possible for defendants to investigate such allegations sufficiently for there to be a reasonable prospect of a fair trial will depend upon a number of factors, not least when the complaint was first made and with what effect. If a complaint has been made and recorded, and more obviously still if the accused has been convicted of the abuse complained of, that will be one thing; if, however, a complaint comes out of the blue with no apparent support for it (other perhaps than that the alleged abuser has been accused or even convicted of similar abuse in the past), that would be quite another thing. By no means everyone who brings a late claim for damages for sexual abuse, however genuine his complaint may in fact be, can reasonably expect the court to exercise the s.33 discretion in his favour. On the contrary, a fair trial (which must surely include a fair opportunity for the defendant to investigate the allegations – see s.33(3)(b)) is in many cases likely to be found quite simply impossible after a long delay.

Following on from that Lord Clarke in *AB v Nugent Care Society*[167c] had commented that there are now likely to be many cases in which a judge will consider that it is not feasible to decide the issues simply by reference to the pleadings, written witness statements and the extent and content of discovery. He or she may well conclude that it is desirable that such oral evidence as is available should be heard because the strength of the claimant's evidence is relevant to the way in which the discretion should be exercised. Although it is necessary to take care not to decide the substantive issues before deciding whether to allow the action to proceed, the two factors are inevitably interrelated. Similarly in *Raggett v Society of Jesus Trust of 1929 for Roman Catholic Purposes*[167d] the Court of Appeal held that it was open to the trial judge to hear and determine issues of liability before deciding the s.33 question. What matters is that the judge should properly consider all the relevant factors and be seen to base the conclusion on that consideration. It is not right to say that in any case where liability is established the s.33 criteria should necessarily be exercised in the claimant's favour.

[167a] [2011] EWHC 279.
[167b] At paras 84–87.
[167c] [2009] EWCA Civ 827, [2010] 1 FLR 707, [2009] Fam. Law 1045.
[167d] [2010] EWCA Civ 1002.

Strength of claimant's case

8–054   *At the end of this paragraph, add the following text and footnote:*

For further authority on the relevance (though not decisiveness) of the apparent strength of the claimant's case in a PI context see *Davies v*

Secretary of State for Energy and Climate Change.[169a] However, that case also makes it clear that the court should not do more than consider prospects of success in a very broad sense—a hopeless case is unlikely to be allowed to proceed under s.33, whereas a very strong case may well be a significant factor in a decision to exercise the discretion in favour of the claimant. It is not appropriate for the court considering the s.33 discretion to conduct a mini-trial on liability.

[169a] [2012] EWCA Civ 1380.

Two claim forms

At the end of this paragraph, add the following text and footnote: **8–058**

Aktas v Adepta (a registered charity); Dixie v British Polythene Industries Plc[176a] concerned the exercise of the s.33 discretion in a case where the claim form was issued on the last day of the three-year limitation period and was not served in time, despite the grant of an extension of time. A second claim form was issued, but this was outside the limitation period and the claimant sought the exercise of the s.33 discretion. The defendant argued that the second claim form was an abuse of process, but the Court of Appeal disagreed. The s.33 discretion is unfettered, and it is not an abuse of process either to fail to serve the first claim form in time or to issue a second claim.

[176a] [2010] EWCA Civ 1170, [2011] 2 All E.R. 536.

DEFAMATION

Extension of time in defamation cases

The conditions of the extension

At the end of this paragraph, add the following text and footnotes: **8–073**

Brady v Norman[207a] considered the relationship between *Steedman v BBC*[207b] and *Cain v Francis.*[207c] The former is a case on s.32A, relevant to defamation, whereas the latter concerns s.33, relevant only to personal injuries. The point raised was that both cases are about the exercise of the discretion to disapply the limitation period, but that they appear to advocate different and possibly inconsistent approaches on the specific question of whether the loss of the limitation defence which will result from the application of the discretion in favour of the claimant is a factor to be taken into account. The Court of Appeal[207d] made the point that considerations in defamation cases are likely to be rather different from those in personal injury cases.

In a personal injury case where the defendant has had proper opportunity to investigate the facts and has admitted liability, the loss of a fortuitous windfall limitation defence will often, depending on the facts, be regarded as of little or no prejudicial weight and likely to be outweighed by the prejudice of the claimant in accidentally losing his claim. Considerations in defamation claims are likely to be different. The policy behind the much shorter limitation period is clear. The defamatory impact of libel or slander is likely to be transient and Parliament evidently intended that a claimant should assert and pursue his need for vindication speedily. As Hale L.J. said in *Steedman*, it is for claimants to make out a case for the disapplication of the normal rule. *Steedman v BBC* and *Cain v Francis* do not articulate different and conflicting principles. They represent differing manifestations of the application of the same principles to be derived from the different circumstances to which adjacent sections of the 1980 Act are applicable.

[207a] [2011] EWCA Civ 107.
[207b] [2001] EWCA Civ 1534.
[207c] [2009] Q.B. 754.
[207d] At para.21.

8–076　*At the end of this paragraph, add the following text and footnote:*

The apparent strength of the claimant's case is a relevant factor in deciding whether or not to exercise the discretion to extend time[214a] (in defamation).

[214a] *Zinda v Ark Academies (Schools)* [2011] EWHC 3394 (QB), Eady J.

CHAPTER 10

ACCRUAL OF CAUSE OF ACTION IN CONTRACT

RIGHT ACCRUES ON BREACH

At the end of this paragraph, add the following text and footnote:　　　**10–002**
In the absence of an entire contract (which is now a relatively rare phenomenon) it is likely that a cause of action for professional services rendered will accrue in stages as parts of the task are completed. The fact that the claimant is in negotiations with the defendant over the details of his entitlement will not normally prevent time from running.[9a]

[9a] *Smales v Lea* [2011] EWCA Civ 1325.

BREACH A QUESTION OF FACT

At the end of this paragraph, add the following text and footnotes:　　　**10–007**
Whether a claim for demurrage accrues on the completion of discharge of cargo or only on the later date when an invoice is presented depends on the terms of the contract. The relationship between the terms of the charterparty

[23]

and the terms of the sale contract may also be of assistance as a matter of construction.[18a]

In *Legal Services Commission v Henthorn*[18b] Lord Neuberger M.R. commented[18c]:

> "Save where it is the essence of the arrangement between the parties that a sum is not payable until demanded (e.g. a loan expressly or impliedly repayable on demand), it appears to me that clear words would normally be required before a contract should be held to give a potential or actual creditor complete control over when time starts running against him, as it is such an unlikely arrangement for an actual or potential debtor to have agreed."

Although that case concerned a sum of money due under an enactment rather than a cause of action founded on contract, the point made appears to be of relevance also in contractual claims.

[18a] *Glencore Energy (UK) Ltd v Sonol Israel Ltd* [2011] EWHC 2756 (Comm), Beatson J.

[18b] [2011] EWCA Civ 1415. See also Chapter 11.

[18c] At para.31.

ACTIONS TO RECOVER SUMS DUE UNDER STATUTE

SUM OF MONEY DUE

At the end of this paragraph, add the following text and footnotes: **11–003**

In *Child Maintenance and Enforcement Commission v Mitchell* [7a] justices had made a liability order against the defendant in relation to child maintenance arrears. When the sums which had formed the basis of the orders remained unpaid, application was made under s.39 of the Child Support Act 1991, which permits the court to disqualify the defendant from driving and/or to commit him to prison. The defendant argued that the application was statute-barred because the liability order was more than six years old. The Court of Appeal rejected this argument. The application was not an action on a judgment, so s.24 of the Limitation Act 1980 did not apply. Nor was it an action to recover a sum due under an enactment because neither of the remedies allowed under s.39 involved the payment of money. It made no difference that an indirect result of the making of an order might be that some or all of the arrears were recovered.

Bolsover DC v Ashfield Nominees Ltd [7b] concerns winding-up petitions based on council tax liability orders. A liability order can be made in respect of tax which has accrued due in the six years before the making of the order, [7c] but thereafter a winding-up petition based on the liability orders is not an action to recover a sum of money due under an enactment within s.9 of the Limitation Act 1980. It may be noted that if council tax is due and unpaid, it is regarded as a debt for the purposes of insolvency proceedings even if a liability order has not yet been made. [7d] That follows the position as regards the old system of rating. [7e] Under that regime it was held [7f] that if the amount in question had been due and unpaid for more than six years, it was time-barred and therefore could not found the basis of a petition. By contrast, if the council uses the option of ordinary civil proceedings to recover arrears of non-domestic rates, the claim would be subject to s.9 of the Limitation Act, and only the last six years' arrears could be recovered. However, the vital point is that the arrears covered by the liability order are recoverable by virtue of that order, not by virtue of any statute. Consequently, s.9 cannot apply.

[7a] [2010] EWCA Civ 333.

[7b] [2010] EWCA Civ 1129.

[7c] Council Tax (Administration and Enforcement) Regulations 1992 (SI 1992/613).

[7d] *Dennis Rye Ltd v Bolsover DC* [2009] EWCA Civ 972.

[7e] *Re North Bucks Furniture Depositories Ltd* [1939] Ch. 690, [1939] 2 All E.R. 549, 37 L.G.R. 371; *Re McGreavy* [1950] Ch. 269, [1950] 1 All E.R. 442, 48 L.G.R. 247.

[7f] *Re Karnos Property Co Ltd* (1988) 87 L.G.R. 263, [1989] B.C.L.C. 340, 5 B.C.C. 14, following *China v Harrow UDC* [1954] 1 Q.B. 178, [1953] 2 All E.R. 1296, 51 L.G.R. 681.

ACCRUAL OF CAUSE OF ACTION

11–012   *At the end of this paragraph, add the following text and footnotes:*

Legal Services Commission v Henthorn[29a] was a case in which the LSC sought repayment from a barrister of sums said to have been overpaid to her on account of Legal Aid Work. Such claims were expressly provided for under the relevant Legal Aid Regulations, and the question was when time began to run for the bringing of the claim. The Court of Appeal held that time did not run until the assessment of the sums due had been completed. This was because that is the earliest date at which the balance due can be ascertained. It rejected the defendant's argument that time ran from the date when the work covered by the relevant Legal Aid Certificate was completed. It also rejected the claimant's alternative argument that time did not run until demand was made for the payment, even though the relevant regulations made the sums payable 'on demand'. The requirement for a demand was treated as a purely procedural matter, rather than as something going to the accrual of the cause of action. There was also discussion of *Central Electricity Generating Board v Halifax Corporation*[29b] and *Swansea City Council v Glass*.[29c] In those two cases, the court held that there was a difference between the date the claim arose and the date from which it was actionable, but in all such cases it is a question of construction of the relevant instrument, whether statute, regulations, rules or contract, in each case as to whether there is such a difference.

[29a] [2011] EWCA Civ 1415.

[29b] [1963] A.C. 785, [1962] 3 All E.R. 915, 61 L.G.R. 125.

[29c] [1992] Q.B. 844, [1992] 2 All E.R. 680, 90 L.G.R. 265.

CHAPTER 13

REAL PROPERTY

LAND

The Land Registration Act 2002

At the end of this paragraph, add the following text and footnotes: **13–005**

Baxter v Mannion[2a] concerned the procedure for correcting the Land Register on the ground of 'mistake'.[2b] The defendant had succeeded in getting himself registered as titleholder on the basis of adverse possession when in fact he was not so entitled. This resulted mainly from the claimant's failure to fill in the relevant forms correctly for objecting to the defendant's registration. The claimant sought rectification, but the defendant argued that there was no relevant 'mistake' because the expression should be limited to procedural mistake by the Registry. The Court of Appeal rejected this, observing that the procedure introduced by the Land Registration Act 2002 allowed only a short time for titleholders to object to applications by others on the basis of adverse possession. Moreover, the Act allows a person to apply on that basis where he has been in possession of a registered estate. It would be invidious to hold that a person who had been wrongly registered could defeat a rectification application simply on the basis that the proper owner had not responded quickly enough. Although the implication of this decision is by no means limited to cases of adverse possession, it does appear to have particular significance in this context.

[2a] [2011] EWCA Civ 120.
[2b] Land Registration Act 2002 Sch.4.

Definition

13–006   *At the end of this paragraph, add the following text and footnotes:*
In *R (on the application of Smith) v Land Registry (Peterborough Office)*[2c]
the Court of Appeal held that it is impossible to acquire title to any part of
the highway by adverse possession. The claimant had relied on a number of
authorities, including *Haigh v West*,[2d] though that case is really about the
acquisition of title by the then highway authority, and *Seddon v Smith*,[2e]
which appears to be about a private right of way rather than a public
highway. Also cited were *Dawes v Hawkins*[2f] and *Harvey v Truro RDC*.[2g]
Dawes v Hawkins is important because it contains the earliest reported
appearance of the maxim "once a highway always a highway", which Byles
J. explained as meaning:

> "for, the public cannot release their rights, and there is no extinctive presumption or pre-
> scription. The only methods of legally stopping a highway are, either by the old writ of *ad
> quod damnum*, or by proceedings before magistrates under the statute."[2h]

It is noticeable that the ways of extinguishing a highway are not stated to
include adverse possession. *Harvey v Truro RDC* also supports the idea that
mere disuse of a highway cannot deprive the public of their rights.[2i]

[2c] [2010] EWCA Civ 200.
[2d] [1893] 2 Q.B. 19, CA.
[2e] (1877) 36 L.T. 168, CA.
[2f] (1860) 25 J.P. 502, 8 C.B.N.S. 848.
[2g] [1903] 2 Ch. 638, Joyce J.
[2h] At p.858.
[2i] See also *Suffolk CC v Mason* [1979] AC 705 at p.710, [1979] 2 All E.R.
369, 77 L.G.R. 621 per Lord Morris of Borth-y-Gest.

Relevance of intention

Presumption of possession

13–036   *At the end of this paragraph, add the following text and footnote:*
Port of London Authority v Ashmore[67a] has now reached the Court of
Appeal. Before the Court of Appeal the argument had developed in two
significant ways from what was argued at first instance. First, the claimant
had accepted that acquisition of title to the river bed by adverse possession
was in principle possible; second, it had been realised that the form of the
question went rather beyond anything which could be necessary to the
decision of the case—not least because it would have applied to vessels
moored in the middle of the river rather than on the riverbank, as the
defendant's vessel was.
The Court of Appeal set aside the part of the declaration referred to
above and remitted the matter for trial on the question whether the defendant had in fact acquired such title, commenting that the matter had not

really been suitable for a preliminary issue. Although the case cannot be regarded as deciding that the acquisition of such title is possible (because the point had been conceded before the hearing in the Court of Appeal) it does seem likely that this conclusion will be reached if it is ever necessary to decide the point.

[67a] [2010] 1 All E.R. 1139, [2010] EWCA Civ 30.

Registered land

At the end of this paragraph, add the following text and footnotes: **13–064**

Swan Housing Association Ltd v Gill[129a] establishes some important procedural points about the workings of the adverse possession rules under the Land Registration Act 2002. Deciding whether adverse possession has been established is in the first instance a task for the Land Registry, rather than for the court, and the correct way to proceed is by an application to the Land Registry.[129b] Secondly, no limitation period runs against the proprietor of a registered title.[129c]

[129a] [2012] EWHC 3129 (QB), Eady J.
[129b] LRA 2002 Sch.6, para.1(1).
[129c] LRA 2002 s.96.

CHAPTER 14

TRUSTEES AND PERSONAL REPRESENTATIVES

BREACH OF TRUST

Section 21(2)(b)

At the end of this paragraph, add the following text and footnotes: **14–007**

In *Kleanthous v Paphitis*,[31a] a case involving a derivative action under the Companies Act 2006, Newey J. commented on the distinction between class 1 and class 2 constructive trusts expounded by Millett L.J. in *Paragon Finance Plc v D B Thakerar & Co.*[31b] In that case, Millett L.J. suggested, without actually deciding, that s.21 of the Limitation Act 1980 does not extend to class 2 constructive trusts. In *Gwembe Valley Development Co Ltd v Koshy (No.3)*,[31c] the Court of Appeal concluded that the trust at issue in that case was "a class 2 trust, within Millett LJ's classification" (para.119), with the result that the claim could not be brought within s.21(1)(b) of the Limitation Act 1980 but apparently assumed that s.21(1)(a) could apply in the case of a class 2 constructive trust. That assumption was later called into question in *Halton International Inc v Guernroy Ltd*[31d] by Carnwath L.J., who had been party to the decision in *Gwembe Valley*. On that basis Newey

J. took the view that in future higher courts are likely to decide that no part of s.21 applies to a class 2 constructive trust.

[31a] [2011] EWHC 2287 (Ch).
[31b] [1999] 1 All E.R. 400, 1 I.T.E.L.R. 735, CA.
[31c] [2003] EWCA Civ 1048, [2004] 1 B.C.L.C. 131.
[31d] [2006] EWCA Civ 801.

FIDUCIARY DUTIES

14–015 *At the end of this paragraph, add the following text and footnotes:*
Further interesting consideration of the difficulties of construing s.21 is to be found in the judgment of Supperstone J. in *Williams v Central Bank of Nigeria*.[49a] After referring to the comments of Millett L.J. in the *Paragon Finance* case (above) he went on to consider the decision of the Hong Kong Court of Final Appeal in *Peconic Industrial Development Ltd v Lau Kwok Fai*.[49b] Lord Hoffmann N.P.J. specifically considered whether one category of non-fiduciaries, namely persons who dishonestly assist a trustee in a fraudulent breach of trust, should be treated in the same way as the trustee and not allowed a limitation defence. He took the view that this could not be the law, because the principle of s.21 is that the limitation defence is denied to fiduciaries, whereas dishonest assisters are not fiduciaries.

In the same case the Hong Kong Court also considered the argument that, as a matter of construction, a claim against a dishonest assister may be within s.21 because it is 'in respect of', in the sense of being accessory to, the actual trustee's fraudulent breach of trust.[49c] But Lord Hoffmann said that in the context of s.21 the words 'in respect of' simply mean that the beneficiary must be claiming against the trustee on the ground that he has committed a fraudulent breach of trust. If it had been intended to include claims against dishonest assisters or other non-fiduciaries on the ground that they were accessories to the breach of trust, the language would have been a good deal clearer. The same view was taken by Mr Richard Sheldon QC, sitting as a deputy High Court Judge in *Cattley v Pollard*.[49d]

However, in the English case of *Statek Corporation v Alford*[49e] Evans-Lombe J. reached the opposite conclusion.[49f] In *Williams v Central Bank of Nigeria*[49g] the Court of Appeal disagreed with Lord Hoffmann's view. Having examined the legislative history, the court accepted that the drafting of s.21 is problematic and that there appears to be no interpretation which can be regarded as entirely satisfactory. However, the court held that the preferable view was that the section applies to disapply the limitation period in any case where the action is in respect of trust property, whether or not it is against anyone who can properly be regarded as a trustee.

[49a] [2011] EWHC 876 (QB).
[49b] [2009] 5 HKC 135.
[49c] This possibility was considered by Danckwerts J. in *GL Baker Ltd v Medway Building and Supplies Ltd* [1958] 1 W.L.R. 1216 at p.1222.
[49d] [2006] EWHC 3130 (Ch), [2007] 2 All E.R. 1086, [2007] 3 W.L.R. 317.
[49e] [2008] EWHC 32 (Ch), [2008] B.C.C. 266.

[49f] See also Mitchell, "Dishonest Assistance, Knowing Receipt, and the Law of Limitation" [2008] 3 Conveyancer and Property Lawyer 226.
[49g] [2012] EWCA Civ 415.

CONTRIBUTION

WHAT MUST BE AGREED?

At the end of this paragraph, add the following text and footnote: **15–018**

Lewis v Scott[23a] concerned the interrelation between s.10(3) and (4) of the Civil Liability (Contribution) Act 1978. A payment had been made by the defendant to the original claimant. Then judgment was given against the party who claimed contribution without final agreement as to the overall level of settlement. The question was whether time ran from the date of the payment or the date when the final settlement level was agreed. At first instance it was held that time ran only from the date of the judgment. An application for permission to appeal was adjourned for the respondent to be heard, but Mummery L.J. expressed the view that the judgment at first instance was probably correct.

[23a] [2010] EWCA 1016.

ARBITRATION

EXTENDING THE TIME-LIMITS

Exercising the section 12 discretion

At the end of this paragraph, add the following text and footnotes: **16–017**

The exercise of the s.12 discretion was further considered in *Willia McIlroy Swindon Ltd v Quinn Insurance Ltd.*[30a] Edwards-Stuart J. was not convinced that he had any power to extend time on the facts of the case (because he considered that the proper seat of the arbitration was Ireland) but nevertheless expressed some views as to what he would have done if he had had jurisdiction. Relying also on the decision of Hamblen J. in *SOS Corporacion Alimentaria SA v Inerco Trade SA*[30b] he noted that the concept of undue hardship under the former legislation had been given a broad meaning and relatively benevolent application that is no longer appropriate under s.12 of the 1996 Act. So far as s.12(3)(b) is concerned in the absence of unusual circumstances, the conduct of the party resisting the application must have been such as to have in some way caused or contributed to the failure of the applicant to comply with the relevant time bar. This point was re-emphasised in *Lantic Sugar Ltd v Baffin Investments*[30c] and *Anglian Water Services Ltd v Laing O'Rourke Utilities Ltd.*[30d]

[30a] [2010] EWHC 2448 (TCC), Edwards-Stuart J.
[30b] [2010] EWHC 162 (Comm), [2010] 2 Lloyd's Rep. 345.
[30c] [2009] EWHC 3325 (Comm), Gross J.
[30d] [2010] EWHC 1529 (TCC), Edwards-Stuart J.

CHAPTER 17

MISCELLANEOUS CASES

CHARGING ORDERS

At the end of this paragraph, add the following text and footnote:　　　　**17–005**

There is no requirement to obtain the permission of the court in order to make a charging order application based on a judgment which is more than six years old.[18a]

[18a] *Fraenkl-Rietti v Cheltenham & Gloucester Plc*, unreported, April 14, 2011, CA.

COMPANY, INSOLVENCY AND BANKRUPTCY LAW

Bankruptcy and insolvency

Administration orders

At the end of this paragraph, add the following text and footnote:　　　　**17–022**

The administrator of a company has no power, without the consent of creditors generally, to admit to proof statute-barred debts. The position is not the same as in a liquidation, which stops the running of time for debts which are not statute-barred at the date of liquidation and replaces it with a statutory scheme for the payment of debts.[51a]

[51a] *Leyland Printing Co Ltd (in administration) v Leyprint Ltd (in administration)* [2010] EWHC 2105 (Ch), Judge Hodge QC. For earlier cases on the point see: *Re Art Reproduction Co Ltd* [1952] Ch. 89, [1951] 2

All E.R. 984, [1951] 2 T.L.R. 979, Wynn-Parry J.; *Re Cases of Taffs Well Ltd* [1992] Ch. 179 at 190B, [1992] B.C.L.C. 11, [1991] 3 W.L.R. 731, Judge Paul Baker QC; *Re Maxwell Fleet and Facilities Management Ltd* [1999] 2 B.C.L.C. 721, especially at pp.725–727, Jules Sher QC; *Re Cosslett (Contractors) Ltd* [2004] EWHC 658 (Ch) at para.31 per Patten J.

Other applications under the Insolvency Act 1986

17–038   *At the end of this paragraph, add the following text and footnote:*
The Insolvency Act s.283A creates a three-year limitation period from the date of the bankruptcy for the trustee to decide what, if anything, to do about any interest in a house which is the home of the bankrupt, the bankrupt's spouse or civil partner, or a former spouse or civil partner of the bankrupt. If the trustee does not take any action of a kind specified in the section within the three-year period, then the bankrupt's former interest ceases to be part of the bankrupt's estate and vests in the bankrupt. This effectively qualifies the 12-year period for setting aside transactions at undervalue under s.339.[78a]

[78a] *Stonham (trustee in bankruptcy of Sebastian Satyanard Ramrattan) v Ramrattan* [2011] EWCA Civ 119.

17–040   *At the end of this paragraph, add the following text and footnote:*
Re Broadside Colours and Chemicals Ltd; Brown v Button[81a] reaffirms the rule that s.212 is a procedural section which does not have a limitation period separate from that of the underlying claim.

[81a] [2011] EWHC 1034 (Ch), Judge Behrens.

CHAPTER 18

ACKNOWLEDGEMENT AND PART-PAYMENT

DEBTS, ETC.

Meaning of "liquidated claim"

At the end of this paragraph, add the following text and footnote:　　　　**18–006**

In *Phillips & Co v Bath Housing Co-operative Ltd*[9a] the Court of Appeal held that a claim by solicitors for remuneration, even though not yet fixed by assessment or otherwise, was within the phrase "debt or other liquidated pecuniary claim" within s.29(5)(a) of the Act. It is a debt claim even if it is not for a liquidated sum because it is not quantified unless and until it is either assessed by the court or agreed by the client or was the subject of a judgment. Consequently, such a claim is capable of being acknowledged within the meaning of s.29 of the Limitation Act 1980. A letter from the client in September 2004 had amounted to saying "we owe you something", inasmuch as it had referred to the claim and had taken issue, or had indicated that issue was to be taken, with the amount claimed, but not with the principle that something had been payable. This was to be treated as a sufficient acknowledgement for the purposes of the section.

[9a] [2012] EWCA Civ 1591.

PART-PAYMENT

18–033 *At the end of this paragraph, add the following text and footnote:*
Where a payment is made on a debt, that is, in the absence of anything more, sufficient to set time running afresh in relation to the whole of the debt, even where the debtor makes it clear that the debt in disputed in part. The proposition, derived from the decision of Kerr J. in *Surrendra Overseas Ltd v Government of Sri Lanka*,[87a] that where it has been made clear that part of the claim is disputed, any acknowledgment relates only to the undisputed balance does not apply to part-payments.

[87a] [1977] 2 All E.R. 481.

DISABILITY

MEANING OF DISABILITY

Infancy

At the end of this paragraph, add the following text and footnote:　　　　**19–003**
    It should be noted that the changes to the definition of "disability" made firstly by the Mental Health Act 2000 and, since 2007, by the Mental Capacity Act 2005, may raise the question of which definition is to be applied in any given case. In *Seaton v Seddon*[3a] it was held that the appropriate definition is the one applicable when the cause of action accrues.

    [3a] [2012] EWHC 735 (Ch), Eady J.

Unsound mind

19–004   *At the end of this paragraph, add the following text and footnote:*

Also in *Seaton v Seddon*[5a] it was held that where the claimant lacks capacity on his 18th birthday, the protection afforded by disability continues seamlessly until such time, if ever, as the lack of capacity ceases.

[5a] See above.

Other incapacities

19–009   *At the end of this paragraph, add the following text and footnotes:*

In *Maga (by his Litigation Friend, the Official Solicitor to the Senior Courts) v Trustees of the Birmingham Archdiocese of the Roman Catholic Church*[17a] (a case of sexual abuse by a priest) the trial judge, relying on two decisions of the Court of Appeal, *Kirby v Leather*[17b] and *Masterman-Lister v Brutton*,[17c] as well as from two first-instance decisions, *White v Fell*,[17d] and *Lindsay v Wood*,[17e] took the view that in determining whether the claimant was under a disability, he needed to consider only one question, namely whether the claimant was able to conduct the instant proceedings, in the sense of being "able to deal rationally with the problems which ... will arise in the course of it", as, if he was not, it was common ground that his inability was by reason of mental disorder. The Court of Appeal, without actually departing from this formulation, expressed some doubt as to whether it was precisely correct.

[17a] [2010] EWCA Civ 256.

[17b] [1965] 2 Q.B. 367, [1965] 2 All E.R. 441, [1965] 2 W.L.R. 1318.

[17c] [2003] EWCA Civ 70, [2003] 1 W.L.R. 1511.

[17d] Unreported, November 12, 1987.

[17e] [2006] EWHC 2895 (QB).

CHAPTER 20

FRAUD, CONCEALMENT AND MISTAKE

CONCEALMENT

"Relevant to the plaintiff's right of action"

At the end of this paragraph, add the following text and footnote: **20–013**
   The reason why the defendant has committed a particular act or omission
is not normally a fact crucial to the cause of action so as to allow the
claimant to invoke s.32.[34a] It is submitted that this observation needs to be
treated with caution. Clearly there will be cases where a defendant might
have a good reason for acting as he did, a reason which would rebut an
allegation of negligence or other breach of duty. In those cases it will only be
when the claimant knows that the good reason did not exist that he is aware
that he has a cause of action.
   [34a] *Ford & Warren v Warring-Davies* [2012] EWHC 3523 (QB), Coulson J.

Professional negligence cases

At the end of this paragraph, add the following text and footnotes: **20–021**
   Williams v Lishman, Sidwell, Campbell & Price Ltd[59a] involved the alleged
negligence of a financial services adviser and raised the question whether, if,

in a claim in negligence, the first (i.e. first in time) loss which completes the claimant's cause of action is deliberately concealed by the defendant, does that loss remain a "fact relevant to the Plaintiff's right of action" (within s.32(1)) even after the occurrence of a *second* (i.e. second in time) source or head of loss which the defendant has not deliberately concealed? The importance of the issue is that if it does remain a "fact relevant to the Plaintiff's right of action", then time does not even begin to run until the claimant has discovered the concealment or should have discovered it. The Court of Appeal took the view that time would not run until the later date on the assumption (found not to be true in this case) that the facts were as suggested by the claimants.[59b]

[59a] [2010] EWCA Civ 418.
[59b] For a fuller account of this case see (2010) 26 J.P.N. 232.

Section 32(2)

20–023　*At the end of this paragraph, add the following text and footnotes:*
　　In *Robertson v Pritchard*[68a] Etherton L.J., in refusing a renewed application for permission to appeal, commented that:

> "a person in the position of the defendant, who states that he knows that he should do work in accordance with the Building Regulations, must also be taken to know what those building regulations are i.e. to know the provisions of the relevant Building Regulations. Otherwise such a statement would either be meaningless, or of little or no practical effect. In the ordinary course, it must follow that, if he is in fact doing the work in breach of those building regulations, he must know that he is doing so. In such circumstances he is deliberately committing a breach of duty".[68b]

　　Clearly it is possible, though perhaps unlikely, that such a person might not in fact be aware of the relevant rules; but this dictum suggests that the constructive knowledge derived from the fact that he ought to know them will be sufficient to amount to a deliberate commission of a breach of duty.
　　However, in the same case it was also held that the building owner had a responsibility to comply with the Building Regulations and that the exercise by him of due diligence would therefore lead to the discovery of the content of those regulations at a fairly early stage.

[68a] [2011] EWCA Civ 1716.
[68b] At para.30.

MISTAKE

20–032　*At the end of this paragraph, add the following text and footnotes:*
　　A "mistake" within s.32(1)(c) has to relate to an essential element of the claim.[94a] This appears to be in line with the same principle adopted in relation to a "fact relevant to the claim" in s.32(1)(b), as to which see para.20–013.
　　In *Test Claimants in the Franked Investment Income Group Litigation v Commissioners of Inland Revenue*[94b] it was held, after detailed review of the authorities and the issues, that *Phillips-Higgins v Harper* is correct in

deciding that s.32(1)(c) applies only where the mistake is an essential element of the cause of action. Although s.32(1)(c) refers to "relief from the
consequences of a mistake" rather than to an action "based on mistake"
there is no substantive differences between the two provisions in this regard.

[94a] *FJ Chalke Ltd v Commissioners for Her Majesty's Revenue & Customs*
[2010] EWCA Civ 313 at para.42.
[94b] [2012] UKSC 19.

CHAPTER 21

PLEADING QUESTIONS

At the end of this paragraph, add the following text and footnote: **21–001**
Where a claim form has been struck out because it was not served within
the four-month period allowed for service, it is not automatically an abuse
of process to issue a second claim form based on the same cause of action,
even in a personal injuries claim where the second claim will require the
exercise of the court's discretion under s.33 of the Limitation Act 1980.[3a]

[3a] *Aktas v Adepta (a registered charity); Dixie v British Polythene Industries Plc* [2010] EWCA Civ 1170.

CPR 3.4

At the end of this paragraph, add the following text and footnotes: **21–006**
Janov v Morris was further considered in *Baljit Singh Bhandal*[16a] where it
was emphasised that whether the bringing of a second action within the
limitation period after the first one has been struck out is very much a fact-
specific matter of discretion.[16b]

[16a] [2011] EWHC 3018 (Admin), Hickinbottom J.
[16b] See also *Wahab v Khan* [2011] EWHC 908, Briggs J.

CHAPTER 23

SECTION 35

AMBIT OF SECTION 35

"The same or substantially the same facts"

At the end of this paragraph, add the following text and footnotes: **23–013**

Berezovsky v Abramovich[13a] contains interesting discussion of the notion of a 'new cause of action' within CPR 17.4 and s.35 of the Limitation Act 1980. The court held[13b] that a cause of action is that combination of facts which gives rise to a legal right. For example, a cause of action in tort has, as its essential ingredients, a plea of duty, breach of duty and consequent damage to the claimant. If it happens to be the case that an element of one of those essential ingredients is misstated, misdescribed or omitted, it does not mean that a correct statement, description or inclusion is a new cause of action; even if the formal result of such a statement, misdescription or omission might technically be that an unaltered claim would have to be dismissed, that still does not mean that a corrective alteration involves or constitutes a new cause of action.[13c]

So, as Robert Walker L.J. said in *Smith v Henniker-Major*:

"So in identifying a new cause of action the bare minimum of essential facts abstracted from the original pleading is to be compared with the minimum as it would be constituted under the amended pleading."[13d]

It may be that if a claimant, suing in tort, substitutes by amendment a different kind of loss from that originally pleaded, he will be asserting a new cause of action, but that will not always be so. If an act of violence constituting a single breach of duty causes the loss of both a cat and a dog, the claimant would not be substituting a new cause of action if he substituted the word "dog" for the word "cat" but would be relying on the original cause of action which had caused loss. He would be substituting a new loss for the old loss but would not be substituting a new cause of action for the original cause of action. If on the other hand the claimant was relying on a second and distinct act of violence causing a loss at some different time from the loss originally caused to the cat, he would no doubt be relying on a different cause of action.

[13a] [2011] EWCA Civ 153.

[13b] Paragraphs 59 et seq.

[13c] See Brett J. in *Cooke v Gill* (1873) L.R. 8 C.P. 107 at p.116: "'Cause of action' has been held from the earliest time to mean every fact which is material to be proved to entitle the plaintiff to succeed – every fact which the defendant would have a right to traverse."

[13d] [2002] EWCA Civ 762, [2003] Ch. 182 at p.210, [2002] 2 B.C.L.C. 655 at para.96.

23–019   *At the end of this paragraph, add the following text and footnotes:*

Normington v Palmers solicitors[41a] contains consideration of the phrase "new cause of action". Proudman J. cites Park J. in *Hoechst (UK) Limited v IRC*:

"A cause of action in this context is not so much the label attaching to a claimant's claim (for example, 'breach of statutory duty' or 'money paid under a mistake of law'). Rather it is the set of facts which entitles the claimant to relief".[41b]

As well as the classic definitions in *Cooke v Gill*[41c] and *Letang v Cooper*[41d] before concluding that it is not possible simply to lift these classic definitions and read them into the language of s.35. As Sir Iain Glidewell said in *Darlington Building Society v O'Rourke*:

"Where ... the claim is based on a breach of duty, whether arising from contract or in tort, the question whether an amendment pleads a new cause of action requires comparison of the unamended pleading with the amendment proposed in order to determine:

(a)   whether a different duty is pleaded;

(b)   whether the breaches pleaded differ substantially; and where appropriate

(c)   the nature and extent of the damage of which complaint is made."

[41a] [2009] EWHC 2036 (Ch), Proudman J.

[41b] [2003] EWHC 1002 (Ch), at para.24.

[41c] (1873) L.R. 8 C.P. 107 at p.116.
[41d] [1965] 1 Q.B. 232 at pp.232–234, per Diplock L.J.

At the end of this paragraph, add the following text and footnote: **23–020**
It is permissible to serve different particulars of claim against different defendants. It does not follow that those particulars which are served after the first will necessarily introduce a new cause of action for the purposes of s.35 of the Limitation Act 1980.[42a]

[42a] *Biddle v Tetrapak* [2010] EWHC 54 (Ch), Warren J.

CPR PART 19

At the end of this paragraph, add the following text and footnote: **23–026**
In *Irwin v Lynch*[62a] the second claimant was a company of which the first and second defendants were directors. In December 2004, the company went into administration and the first claimant was appointed as administrator. In August 2007, the first claimant issued an ordinary application in his own name that sought relief against the defendants in respect of, inter alia, an alleged transaction at an undervalue and/or misfeasance or breach of trust. In December 2009, the defendants issued a strike out application in respect of those claims on the ground that the first claimant, as administrator, had no locus standi to bring the claim under s.212 of the Insolvency Act 1986 and that the court, therefore, had no jurisdiction to entertain the misfeasance/breach of trust claims. In January 2010, the first claimant applied to amend or substitute the company to the ordinary application in accordance with CPR 17.4(4) and 19.5. The Court of Appeal held that this application should be granted. The company had a meritorious claim against the defendants and that claim could not be maintained unless the company was substituted for the first claimant, following which, the amended claim would be valid and could be maintained successfully. The first claimant had asserted the rights on behalf of the company, not himself, the cause of action was identical and not changed with the change of identity of the party bringing it; however, the action would have failed but for the change in identity as the first claimant did not have locus standi to bring the claim. In those circumstances, it was appropriate for the court to exercise its discretion and allow the substitution of the name of the company for that of the first claimant in accordance with CPR 19.5.

[62a] [2010] All E.R. (D) 118 (Oct), CA.

At the end of this paragraph, add the following text and footnotes: **23–027**
Lockheed Martin Corporation v Willis Group Ltd[63a] concerned substitution of a party on the ground of mistake under CPR19.5. The Court of Appeal discussed, obiter, but in detail and persuasively, the question whether the requirement of the former RSC Ord.20, r.5 that the error in naming the defendant must not have been misleading to the true defendant continued to be the law under CPR, notwithstanding that CPR 19.5 does not replicate this wording. The Court of Appeal's view was that under the current law there is no such requirement, though the question whether the true

defendant has been prejudiced by the mistake may well be a relevant factor in the exercise of the discretion. The mistake which is to be corrected does not have to appear in the *original* claim form. Thus, where the true defendant had been included in the original claim form but wrongly deleted before service, the court could entertain an application to restore that defendant to the proceedings.[63b]

Yet another case on the naming of a party by mistake in the original claim form is *The Insight Group Ltd v Kingston Smith (a firm)*[63c] where a solicitors' negligence claim was brought against the LLP into which the original partnership had transformed itself. Most of the alleged acts of negligence had taken place before the transformation. Leggatt J. held that the LLP could properly be regarded as having been named by mistake, so that there was discretion to allow the substitution of the partnership as defendant.

[63a] [2010] EWCA Civ 927.

[63b] *Standard Life Assurance Ltd v Metsec Plc* [2010] EWHC 2003 (Ch).

[63c] [2012] EWHC 3644 (QB), Leggatt J.

23–030   *At the end of this paragraph, add the following text and footnotes:*

Roberts v Gill & Co (a firm)[74a] concerned amendment of pleadings so as to allow a beneficiary under a will to bring a representative action in addition to a personal action against solicitors for their alleged negligence in the handling of an estate. In the end the majority of the Supreme Court decided the basis on the ground that the claimant had not made out special circumstances such as would justify the exercise of the court's discretion to allow such an amendment. The application had also been resisted on the ground that there was no jurisdiction to make such an amendment under CPR 19.5(3). Although this question was discussed at some length, the Supreme Court deliberately chose not to decide it. The majority view appears to be that it might well not have been absolutely necessary to join the administrator of the estate as a party, although there is no doubt that it is the usual practice. Although the judgments contain extensive discussion of the history of RSC Ord.20, r.5 and now CPR 19.5, in the end the point of this discussion seems to go to a point about the law of derivative actions, rather than a point of limitation.

The point discussed in *Roberts v Gill* was further considered in *Nemeti v Sabre Insurance Co Ltd*,[74b] where it was held that the rules in s.35(5)(b) and (6)(b) allowing the substitution of a new party where this is necessary for the determination of the original action are to be narrowly construed. Thus, where the claimant in a road traffic case had wrongly started proceedings against a motor insurer instead of against the estate of the allegedly negligent driver, his subsequent application to bring in the estate as an additional party did not meet these requirements. Although he could not succeed against the estate without bringing it in, the original action could perfectly well be disposed of without doing so.

[74a] [2010] UKSC 22.

[74b] [2012] EWHC 3355 (QB), Judge Cotter QC.

THE MERCHANT SHIPPING ACT 1995

EXTENDING TIME

Prejudice to defendant

At the end of this paragraph, add the following text and footnotes:　　　　**24–012**

A party wishing to take the point that a claim (here a counterclaim, but nothing turns on that fact) is out of time is expected to do so at the first opportunity.[35a] Failure to do so may result in the court finding that it is too late to take the time-bar point, or that there is an estoppel or that there is good reason to extend time under s.190(5) of the Merchant Shipping Act 1995

In *Gold Shipping Navigation Co SA v Lulu Maritime Ltd*[35b] Teare J. rejected an argument that s.190 of the Merchant Shipping Act 1995 does not apply to counterclaims. Although it had long been settled that s.8 of the Maritime Conventions Act 1911 (the predecessor of s.190) did apply to counterclaims[35c] it was submitted that the 1995 Act did not so apply. Teare J. commented that in passing the 1995 Act Parliament must be taken to have been aware of the interpretation given to s.8 of the 1911 Act and that nothing in the 1995 Act showed a clear intention to change that interpretation.

[35a] *MIOM 1 Ltd v Sea Echo ENE (No.2)* [2011] EWHC 2715 (Admlty), Teare J.

[35b] [2009] EWHC 1365 (Admlty).
[35c] *The Fairplay XIV*—see para.24–017 of the main text.

THE FOREIGN LIMITATION PERIODS ACT 1984

UNDUE HARDSHIP

Prejudice to defendant

At the end of this paragraph, add the following text and footnote: **25–018**
The requirement in s.2(2) of FLPA that the claimant must be disadvantaged by the application of the foreign limitation period is not satisfied where the disadvantage results either from incorrect legal advice given to him or from the uncertainty of the law in the foreign country.[43a]

[43a] *Harley v Smith* [2010] EWCA Civ 78.

THE CARRIAGE STATUTES

SUBSTITUTE TONNAGE

Effect of expiry

At the end of this paragraph, add the following text and footnote: **26–009**
Article III r.6 of the Hague-Visby Rules was considered and applied by analogy in *Röhlig (UK) Ltd v Rock Unique Ltd*[17a] with a reminder that this is a time-bar which extinguishes the substantive right rather than merely barring the remedy.

[17a] [2011] EWCA Civ 18.

CARRIAGE BY AIR ACT 1961

At the end of this paragraph, add the following text and footnote: **26–024**
However, in *More v KLM NV*[47a] the CJEU considered the effect of Regulation 261/2004, which makes provision for compensation for air passengers in the event of delay to their flight. That Regulation contains no provision for time limits for the bringing of proceedings. The Court rejected KLM's argument that in construing this Regulation the applicable time limit should be the same as that in the Warsaw Convention, holding instead that the appropriate period as laid down in the domestic law must apply. It

is to be noted that the Regulation provides compensation simply for delay. Unlike the Warsaw Convention it does not require personal injury or loss or damage to property.

[47a] Case C-139/11, November 22, 2012.

CHAPTER 27

OTHER STATUTES

EQUAL PAY ACT 1970

27–006   *At the end of this paragraph, add the following text and footnote:*
As a general rule an equal pay claim which would be out of time if presented to an Employment Tribunal may instead be brought in the ordinary civil court. Although that court had a discretion to strike out claims which can more conveniently be disposed of separately in the Employment Tribunal, this requirement will not normally be met where the Employment Tribunal would be bound to reject the claim as being out of time.[14a] The decision is at first sight surprising, since, as the minority of the Supreme Court point out, the allocation of these matters to the Employment Tribunal was apparently intended to take them away from the civil courts; on the other hand the legislation does not expressly produce that effect, and there is no doubt that the claims, as breach of contract claims, are within the jurisdiction of the civil courts unless removed by statute.
[14a] *Abdulla v Birmingham CC* [2011] EWCA Civ 1412, affirmed (by a bare majority) by the Supreme Court [2012] UKSC 47.

SEX DISCRIMINATION ACT 1975 AND RACE RELATIONS ACT 1976

Discretion to extend

27–020   *At the end of this paragraph, add the following text and footnotes:*
Biggs v Somerset CC was followed by the First-tier Tax Tribunal in *TC01247: The Trustees of the BT Pension Scheme,*[42a] where it was observed that the decision seemed to be supported also by *HMRC v Marks & Spencer.*[42b] The latter case was also referred to in *BCL Old Co Ltd v BASF SE (sued as BASF AG)*[42c] (discussed below).
[42a] [2011] UKFTT 392 (TC).
[42b] [2010] UKUT 213.
[42c] [2010] EWCA Civ 1258.

PROCEEDS OF CRIME ACT 2002

27–034   *At the end of this paragraph, add the following text and footnotes:*
In *Gale v Serious Organised Crime Agency*[76] the Court of Appeal considered s.27A of the Limitation Act 1980, which creates a limitation period of 12 years for asset-recovery claims under Part 5 of the Proceeds of Crime Act 2002. That period runs from the date on which the cause of action accrues. The cause of action accrues in respect of any recoverable property in the case of proceedings for a recovery order in respect of property obtained through unlawful conduct, when the property is so obtained and in the case of proceedings for a recovery order in respect of any other recoverable property, when the property obtained through unlawful conduct which it represents is so obtained. Curiously, s.316(3) provides: "For the purpose of deciding whether or not property was recoverable at any time (including times before commencement), it is to be assumed that this Part

was in force at that and any other relevant time." Accordingly, it seems, a limitation defence may be relied on against SOCA, even though it depends on events before the assets recovery regime was introduced in 2002, and even though SOCA itself was not created until 2005.[77] In the end the Court of Appeal felt able to decide *Gale* on the basis that the defendants had not been able to make good a limitation defence, perhaps a slightly surprising approach, given the usual rule that once the defendant pleads limitation the burden is on the claimant.

Another interesting case on the Proceeds of Crime Act is *Baljit Singh Bhandal*,[78] which concerned a compensation application by a defendant against whom proceedings had been begun and then discontinued. The Act requires that such an application be brought under CPR Part 23 as an application in the existing civil proceedings for a restraint order against him, rather than as a free-standing action. It was held that s.35 therefore applied to such an application (which has to be treated as the bringing of a new claim), with all the restrictions which that involves. The limitation period begins to run when the warrant in the criminal proceedings is cancelled.

[76] [2010] EWCA Civ 759.
[77] *Director of Assets Recovery Agency v Szepietowski* [2007] EWCA Civ 766 at para.59, per Waller L.J.
[78] [2011] EWHC 3018 (Admin), Hickinbottom J.

Add the following text and footnotes as a new paragraph: **27–036**

Mermec UK Ltd v Network Rail Infrastructure Ltd[79] was a case concerning the Utilities Contracts Regulations 2006. In common with other regulations in the field of public procurement these Regulations impose a short limitation period of three months for the issue (and now also service) of proceedings complaining about a public procurement decision, though there is limited discretion to grant an extension of time where there is good reason to do so. The present case concerned the point at which time begins to run. Regulation 45D of the Regulations provides that proceedings must be commenced within three months beginning with the date when grounds for starting the proceedings first arose. The comparable provision in the Public Contracts Regulations (reg.47D) was reviewed in *Sita UK Ltd v Greater Manchester Waste Disposal Authority*[80] by Mann J., who decided that the time period for the institution of proceedings was to be considered as three months from the time when the claiming economic operator knew or ought to have known of the alleged infringements of the Regulations, subject to any extension of that period. That decision was upheld in the Court Appeal, which reviewed a number of authorities including the European Court of Justice decision in *Uniplex (UK) Ltd v NHS Business Services Authority*,[81] where it was held that the mere fact that a candidate or tenderer learns that its application or tender has been rejected does not place it in a position effectively to bring proceedings. Such information is insufficient to enable the candidate or tenderer to establish whether there has been any illegality which might form the subject matter of proceedings. It is only once a concerned candidate or tenderer has been informed of the reasons for its elimination from the public procurement procedure that it may come to an informed view as to whether there has been an infringement of the applicable provisions and as to the appropriateness of bringing proceedings. The difficulty is to know what degree of knowledge is sufficient to provide the necessary informed view that a legal claim lies. That depends upon how certain a case should be before a party is expected to take proceedings. Akenhead J. disagreed with Mann J.'s formulation that "the standard ought to be a knowledge of the facts which apparently clearly indicate, though they need not absolutely prove, an infringement". Instead, he preferred to draw an analogy with the test laid down by the House of Lords in *Haward v Fawcetts (a firm)*[82] which involved a claim for damages in a latent damage case where s.14A of the Limitation Act 1980 applied, namely that:

"... knowledge does not mean knowing for certain and beyond possibility of contradiction. It means knowing with sufficient confidence to justify embarking on the preliminaries to the issue of a writ, such as submitting a claim to the proposed defendant, taking advice, and collecting evidence: 'suspicion, particularly if it is vague and unsupported, will indeed not be enough, but reasonable belief will normally suffice'."[83]

In *BCL Old Co Ltd v BASF SE (sued as BASF AG)*[84] it was held that there is no power under s.47A of the Competition Act 1998 to extend time for bringing an action against members of a cartel.

[79] [2011] EWHC 1847 (TCC), Akenhead J.
[80] [2010] EWHC 680 (Ch), [2010] 2 C.M.L.R. 1283; para.28–018.
[81] [2010] 2 C.M.L.R. 47.
[82] [2006] 1 W.L.R. 682; for that case see para.6–014.
[83] At para.9.
[84] [2010] EWCA Civ 1258; affirmed by the Supreme Court [2012] UKSC 45.

CHAPTER 28

EUROPEAN LAW

EQUAL PAY ACT 1970

Domestic courts

At the end of this paragraph, add the following text and footnote: **28–013**
For the purposes of a follow-on claim under the Competition Act 1998 s.47A for damages against a defendant found guilty of price-fixing, the two-year limitation period runs from when proceedings against all defendants are concluded. There is not a separate limitation period for each defendant. Consequently, time does not run until the conclusion of any appeal process, even against a defendant who does not appeal.[18a]

[18a] *Deutsche Bahn AG v Morgan Crucible Co Plc* [2012] EWCA Civ 1055.

Requirements of promptness

At the end of this paragraph, add the following text and footnotes: **28–018**
The decision of Mann J. in *Sita UK Ltd v Greater Manchester Waste Disposal Authority* has been upheld by the Court of Appeal, though its approach differs somewhat from his.[28a] Subsequently the issues have been further considered in *Turning Point Ltd v Norfolk CC*,[28b] which also referred to *Mermec Ltd v Network Rail Infrastructure Ltd*.[28c] Akenhead J. summarised the current position as follows.
The Court of Appeal in *Sita*[28d] commented that the crucial question is what degree of knowledge or constructive knowledge is required before time begins to run. In other words, when is the information known or constructively known to the appellant sufficient to justify taking proceedings for an infringement of the public procurement requirements? In the Uniplex case[28e] the ECJ said that the fact that a candidate or tenderer learns that its application or tender has been rejected does not place it in a position effectively to bring proceedings. Such information is insufficient to enable

the candidate or tenderer to establish whether there has been any illegality which might form the subject matter of proceedings. It is only once a concerned candidate or tenderer has been informed of the reasons for its elimination from the public procurement procedure that it may come to an informed view as to whether there has been an infringement of the applicable provisions and as to the appropriateness of bringing proceedings.[28f] But what degree of knowledge is sufficient to provide that informed view that a legal claim lies? That depends upon how certain a case should be before a party is expected to take proceedings. Is a claimant expected to initiate proceedings once there is an arguable case, a reasonably arguable case, a strongly arguable case, or even a certain case? He may have knowledge sufficient to enable him to conclude that he has an arguable case but it may not be sufficient to enable him to take an informed view as to whether it is a strong case. So if the latter test is the right one, time will not begin to run until he acquires further knowledge which enables him to take an informed view about that. Mann J.'s formulation was that "the standard ought to be a knowledge of the facts which apparently clearly indicate, though they need not absolutely prove, an infringement."

That puts the test too high. In effect the Court of Appeal in *Sita* held that time starts running when the tenderer has sufficient information to commence proceedings.

The *Mermec* case also provided some guidance on extension. Although it may be unhelpful to try to give some exhaustive list of the grounds upon which extensions should be granted, such grounds would include factors which prevent service of the claim within time which are beyond the control of the claimant; these could include illness or detention of the relevant personnel. There must, however, be a good reason. The fact that the delay is only very short is not a factor which carries great weight. There is no point in having a three-month period if what it means is three months plus a further relatively random short period.

[28a] [2011] EWCA Civ 156.
[28b] [2012] EWHC 2121 (TCC), Akenhead J.
[28c] [2011] EWHC 1847 (TCC).
[28d] At paras 19 et seq., per Elias L.J.
[28e] *Uniplex (UK) Ltd v NHS Business Services Authority* [2010] 2 C.M.L.R. 47.
[28f] *Uniplex* at para.31.

HUMAN RIGHTS

28–036 *At the end of this paragraph, add the following text and footnotes:*

Where the claimant's solicitor had delayed in starting proceedings against the police until the provision of an independent IPCC report, and in the belief that time would not run until that report was received, the Court exercised its discretion to allow a human rights claim out of time. However, comment was also made that the discretion under the HRA is very general, and that it is unwise to seek to argue too closely by analogy with s.33 of the

Limitation Act 1980.[65a] In *Rabone v Pennine Care NHS Foundation Trust*,[65b] Lord Dyson, discussing a similar point said:

"The court has a wide discretion in determining whether it is equitable to extend time in the particular circumstances of the case. It will often be appropriate to take into account factors of the type listed in section 33(3) of the Limitation Act 1980 as being relevant when deciding whether to extend time for a domestic law action in respect of personal injury or death. These may include the length of and reasons for the delay in issuing the proceedings; the extent to which, having regard to the delay, the evidence in the case is or is likely to be less cogent than it would have been if the proceedings had been issued within the one year period; and the conduct of the public authority after the right of claim arose, including the extent (if any) to which it responded to requests reasonably made by the claimant for information for the purpose of ascertaining facts which are or might be relevant. However, I agree with what the Court of Appeal said in *Dunn v Parole Board* [2009] 1 WLR 728, paras 31, 43 and 48 that the words of section 7(5)(b) of the HRA mean what they say and the court should not attempt to rewrite them. There can be no question of interpreting section 7(5)(b) as if it contained the language of section 33(3) of the Limitation Act 1980."[65c]

In *Dobson v Thames Water Utilities Ltd (Water Services Regulation Authority (Ofwat) intervening) (No.2)*[65d] Ramsey J. suggested that the fact that some claimants were infants could be a relevant factor in exercising the discretion to extend time under s.7(5) of the HRA.

[65a] *R. (on the application of D) v Metropolitan Police Commissioner* [2012] EWHC 309 (QB), Eady J.

[65b] [2012] UKSC 2.

[65c] At para.75.

[65d] 140 Con. L.R. 135, [2011] EWHC 3253 (TCC), Ramsey J.

At the end of this paragraph, add the following text and footnotes: **28–037**

Section 19(3) of the Land Compensation Act 1973 has the effect of barring claims for compensation where a highway is not adopted by the highway authority within three years of it first being open to public traffic.[67] In *Thomas v Bridgend CBC*[68] the Court of Appeal held that this rule is an expropriation of property rights not compatible with the ECHR.

[67] See *Price v Caerphilly County Borough Council* [2005] R.V.R. 103 and *O'Connor v Wiltshire County Council* [2006] 2 E.G.L.R. 81.

[68] [2012] Q.B. 512, [2011] EWCA Civ 862.

INDEX

LEGAL TAXONOMY
FROM SWEET & MAXWELL

This index has been prepared using Sweet and Maxwell's Legal Taxonomy. Main index entries conform to keywords provided by the Legal Taxonomy except where references to specific documents or non-standard terms (denoted by quotation marks) have been included. These keywords provide a means of identifying similar concepts in other Sweet & Maxwell publications and online services to which keywords from the Legal Taxonomy have been applied. Readers may find some minor differences between terms used in the text and those which appear in the index. Suggestions to **taxonomy@sweetandmaxwell.co.uk**.